Contents

Weblink: www.curriculumvisions.com

Sounds around us

We hear lots of sounds all the time.

Nearly everything that moves makes a sound.

Dogs howl, water splashes, machines whirr, friends call us on the phone.

The streets buzz with people talking and walking.

A dog makes a sound when it howls or barks.

You hear sounds around the house.

Weblink: www.curriculumvisions.com

Birds sing to each other.

Cities are full of the sounds of people and traffic.

Sit still for one minute.
How many different sounds can you hear?

Weblink: www.curriculumvisions.com

Musical sounds

We make many kinds of sounds with musical instruments.

Music can be a nice sound.

We can make music by singing.

We can make music by playing an instrument.

We can pluck a guitar.

We can blow a recorder.

Weblink: www.curriculumvisions.com

We can play the maracas.

We can tap a tambourine.

We can bang a drum.

We can blow a trumpet.

How do you play your favourite musical instrument?

3 Loud and quiet

Sounds are not all the same.

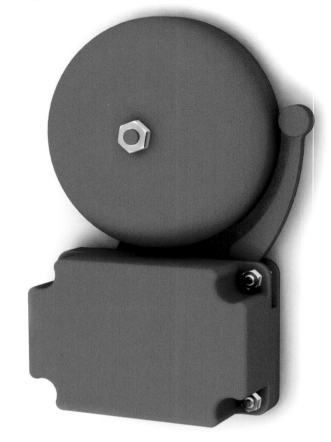

Some sounds are loud.
An alarm bell is loud.

Some sounds are quiet.
A cat purring is a quiet sound.

Loud sounds can be heard
from a long way away.

Quiet sounds can only be
heard if you are very close.

Helicopters make a loud sound.

A fire bell makes
a loud sound.

Weblink: www.curriculumvisions.com

A purring cat makes a quiet sound.

A whisper is a quiet sound.

Turn this page. Do you make a loud or a quiet sound?

Weblink: www.curriculumvisions.com

High and low

Sounds can be high or low.

Some sounds are like squeaks. These are high sounds.

Some sounds are like roars. These are low sounds.

If you squeeze a toy, like a rubber duck, it will make a high sound.

A whistle makes a high sound when you blow it.

Weblink: www.curriculumvisions.com

If you pluck the thin strings of a guitar you will get a high note.

A lion makes a low sound when it roars.

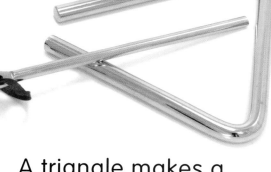

A triangle makes a high sound. It goes "ting" when you hit it.

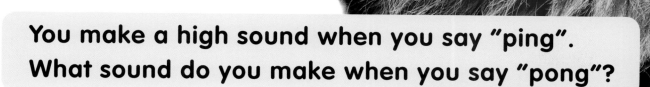

You make a high sound when you say "ping".
What sound do you make when you say "pong"?

5 Sounds you can make

You can make many sounds with your body.

You can clap your hands.

You can stamp your feet.

You can sing.

You can shout.

You can whistle.

You can cry.

You can whistle.

You can clap your hands.

You can tap with your feet.

You can shout.

You can sing.

What other sounds can you make?

Weblink: www.curriculumvisions.com

Ears

We use our ears to hear the sounds around us.

Our ears are shaped like funnels. They take sound into our heads.

It is hard to keep sounds out.

You can hear better by putting your hand behind your ear.

You hear less sound when you are wearing a hood.

Weblink: www.curriculumvisions.com

Earphones make it easy to hear music. But you can harm your ears if you play music too loudly.

Do you still hear sounds when you cover your ears with your hands?

Weblink: www.curriculumvisions.com

Sounds near and far

Sounds seem louder when you are close to them.

When sounds are near they can be loud.

When sounds are far away they seem quiet.

Sounds seem quieter the farther they are from you.

This aeroplane is far away, so it seems quiet.

This aeroplane is close and so it seems much louder.

Weblink: www.curriculumvisions.com

As you walk to a fairground it sounds louder.

This alarm clock sounds loud by your bedside, but quiet if you are outside.

This motorbike seems loud when it is near. As the motorbike goes away it seems quieter.

Bring a ticking watch close to your ear. Does it get louder or quieter?

Weblink: www.curriculumvisions.com

Noise

A noise is a sound that people do not like.

A noise is a sound we don't like.

A noise can be quiet as well as loud.

A quiet noise is someone tapping a desk when we are trying to read.

We can cover our ears to keep out some noise.

Snoring is a noise that can keep us awake.

Weblink: www.curriculumvisions.com

Some people think rock music is a noise.

The sound of traffic can make a noise.

Large digging machines make a noise.

Is cheering a noise?   **Do you like people to cheer you?**

Vibrations

Something vibrates when it shakes very quickly.

If you tap most things they make a dull thud.

Some make a ringing sound.

When something makes a ringing sound, it is shaking about. We say it is vibrating.

We call the shaking a vibration.

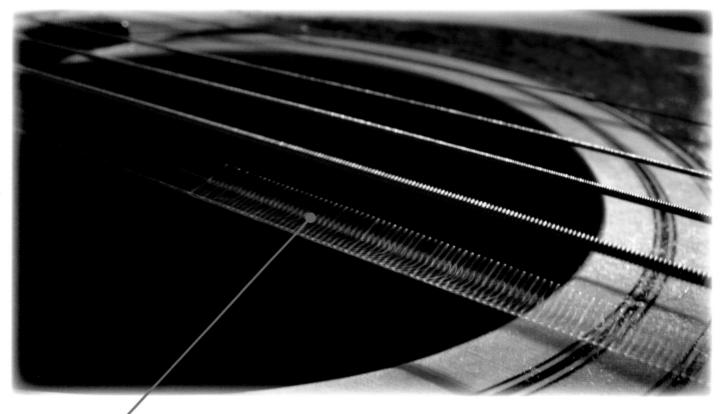

guitar string

You can see guitar strings shake to and fro when you pluck them.

Weblink: www.curriculumvisions.com

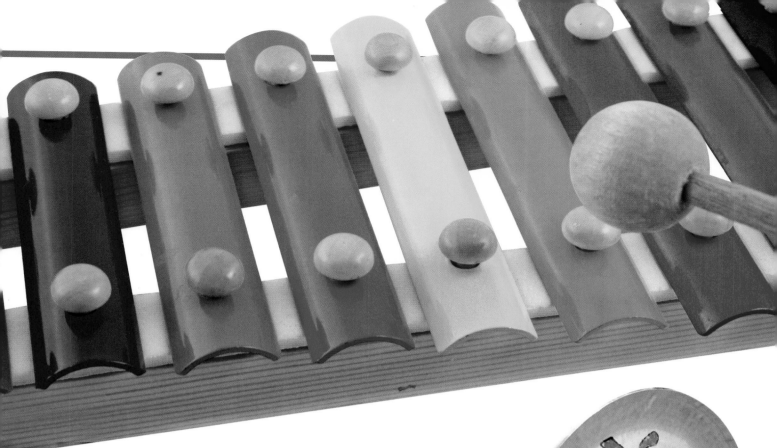

You can watch the bars on a xylophone shaking about when you hit them.

A bell vibrates when it is rung.

cymbals

You can feel your hands shake when you crash cymbals together.

Can you feel your lips vibrate when you blow a raspberry?

Weblink: www.curriculumvisions.com

Words to learn

Cities

Places bigger than towns where lots of people live and work.

Cymbals

A pair of thin round metal instruments which are banged together to make a sound.

Earphones

Small loudspeakers that are worn on the ears.

Fire bell

A bell that rings to warn people there is a fire which could be dangerous.

Weblink: www.curriculumvisions.com

Funnel

An object shaped like a cone with an opening at each end.

funnel

Maracas

A pair of rattles with pebbles or beans inside them.

Snoring

Noisy breathing when someone is asleep.

Traffic

Cars, lorries and buses moving along a road.

Triangle

A metal instrument with three sides which makes a ringing sound.

Weblink: www.curriculumvisions.com

Index